When They V

Growing

Simone Biles

by Angela Gail Griffin

Owl Moon Press

When They Were Kids

Growing Up As…Simone Biles

By Angela Gail Griffin

Cover art by Valerie Valdivia, valerievaldivia.com
Chapter art by Vajihe Golmazari, www.vajihegolmazari.com
Edited by David Aretha

"When They Were Kids" is a series of biographies on icons and legends, both contemporary and historical. The purpose of the series is to inform, enlighten, entertain, and inspire young middle-grade readers, as well as to help improve their reading skills and cultivate a joy for reading.

This is a work of nonfiction. No names have been changed, no characters invented, no events fabricated.

We make every effort to properly fact-check the text while relying on only trusted sources, and we try to avoid any claims that might be deemed disparaging. If you notice any facts that you believe are or might be inaccurate, please email us at daretha@live.com and, if you are correct, we will update the book.

Owl Moon Press
www.owlmoonpress.com

ISBN 979-8-9898313-7-1

Contents

Chapter 1

"Simone, You Can Fly!"

Three-year-old Simone and her five-year-old brother, Tevin, loved playing on the backyard swing set, pushing themselves higher and higher until it was time to jump. But Tevin didn't just leap off the swing; he did backflips off it. Little Simone watched her older brother soar through the air and thought if Tevin could do it, she could too.

The first time Simone flipped off the swing, she shot up even higher than Tevin did. He could hardly believe his eyes. As Simone flew bottom-side-up and landed in the soft grass, Tevin yelled, "Simone, you can fly! You can fly!"

Simone adored her big brother. She followed him wherever he went, observing everything he did. If Tevin somersaulted and cartwheeled, Simone tumbled and spun through the air with him. If Tevin raced through the yard, Simone was close behind him. If Tevin hopped like a bunny, Simone hopped even higher.

Many nights, Simone sneaked into the boys' room to snuggle with Tevin even though her foster mother, Miss Doris, told her not to do it. Morning after morning, Miss Doris discovered Simone in Tevin's bed, and each time, she reminded Simone to sleep in the girls' room in her bed. But night after night, Simone disobeyed her foster mom and sneaked into Tevin's room. In her Facebook Watch Series, *Simone vs. Herself,* Simone recalled sleeping with Tevin "because I thought in the morning he was going to disappear."

Simone, Tevin, and their two sisters lived with their foster parents, Miss Doris and Mr. Leo. They did so because their mother was not taking good care of them. Miss Doris and Mr. Leo were nice enough, Simone thought, but they did not feel like her family. Tevin was Simone's real family, and she refused to allow Miss Doris to keep her from him. Simone felt safe and loved when she was with Tevin. She has called him her "rock" and her "protector."

Simone could do anything Tevin could do with her lightning-fast legs and strong muscles. By the time she was in the third grade, Simone's muscles were more noticeable than the other kids'. Her classmates made fun of her and called her a *swoldger,* a combination of *swollen* and *soldier*. Simone did not like it when the kids called her a *swoldger*; she thought it was a mean thing to say. In a letter Simone wrote to "teenage girls everywhere," she explained how she felt about being different:

And remember, if there's something about you that makes you different from those around you, own it. I used to feel awkward and shy about my muscular body because none of the girls at school had a figure like mine. I found that hard to accept, so I'd always wear jackets to hide my muscles. But now I love it. I figure I was born with this body for a reason, so I'm going to use it.

Simone Biles' decision to accept and use her body is why she became the greatest of all time, the G-O-A-T, in gymnastics. Simone won her first United States gymnastics all-around title at 16. She would win eight more all-around

U.S. titles: in 2014, 2015, 2016, 2018, 2019, 2021, 2023, and 2024. In October 2023, Simone won her sixth all-around World Championships gold medal. As of 2024, Simone holds the record for the most international gymnastics medals: 30 World medals (23 gold) and seven Olympic medals (four gold).

Simone's gymnastics career could have abruptly ended when she withdrew from the women's team event at the 2020 Summer Olympics in Tokyo, Japan. Twenty-four-year-old Simone had no problem with her routines before going to the Olympics. But the day after the preliminary rounds in Tokyo, she felt something was severely wrong. And it was too late for the team to choose an alternate gymnast to replace her.

During the team competition, Simone got lost in the air while performing her vault and did not complete her last rotation. Her brain was not connecting with her body. Instead of landing firmly on her feet, Simone stumbled and took a giant step forward. She was lucky she landed upright and not on her head or back. Fighting back tears, she left the competition floor with the team doctor as her teammates stood dazed and confused.

When Simone returned, Team USA had gathered around the uneven bars after completing their vault rotation.

Simone was wearing her hand grips (a device to help the gymnast hold onto the bars) and appeared ready to warm up with the team. But, instead of taking her turn on the bars, Simone removed her grips, put on her warm-up suit, and told the girls she was pulling out of the team competition.

Simone described that moment during an interview with the NBC TV show *Today*: "They were like crying, and I was like, 'You guys need to relax; you're going to be fine without me. Go out there, kick some butt just like you've done in training, and just lay it out on the floor and see what happens. I've been to the Olympics before, and I'll be fine.'"

Simone was suffering from a dangerous condition known as the *twisties*. When gymnasts get the twisties, they can no longer sense where their body is in the air or how far it is from the ground. "Literally cannot tell up from down. It's the craziest feeling ever, not having an inch of control over your body. What's even scarier is since I have no idea where I am in the air, I also have NO idea how I'm going to land or what I'm going to land on head/hands/feet/back..." Simone posted on one of her Instagram stories.

Simone's teammates supported her decision to put her safety first and withdraw from the competition. They fought courageously without her, but

Team USA's final score was not high enough to beat the Russians. With a second-place silver medal gleaming on her chest, Simone commented: "We'll just take this and cherish this forever. This medal is all theirs." Even though Simone competed in only one event, she was still eligible for the team medal.

Simone could have taken her silver medal and gone home after the team competition. But, the determined "swoldger" was not ready to give up. Simone believes "a person can only fail if they stop trying, if they refuse to pick themselves up and try harder."

On the last day of the gymnastics competition at the Tokyo Olympics,

Simone Biles, the G-O-A-T, picked herself back up onto the balance beam for the individual event finals. It was her only chance to win another medal before returning home. She could not dismount with the double twisting double flip named after her because the twisties had not disappeared. Instead, Simone did a double pike, a dismount she had not done since she was 12. Although her routine was not what she had planned, it was good enough to win the bronze medal, which Simone says means as much as all the gold ones.

After two years of therapy sessions and exercises to help her regain control in the air, Simone Biles competed for the first time since the Tokyo Olympics at the U.S. Classic in 2023. Before the Classics, Simone shared she was fine and twisting again. And twist again she did! Simone won the gold medal for the best all-around gymnast!

"It felt really good, especially after everything that's happened over the past year," Biles told NBC. "Everyone that was cheering made posters and all of that. It just made my heart melt that they still believe in me."

Simone Biles' fans have never stopped believing in her. They have witnessed her perform some of the most advanced skills ever executed in women's gymnastics. Five are named after her: two on vault, two on floor exercise, and one on balance beam.

Simone was born to be a gymnast. Her four-foot-eight-inch, 104-pound muscular body is the perfect size for a female gymnast. The smaller a gymnast is, the easier it is to spin, rotate, and fly through the air.

Not only was Simone born with a perfect gymnastics body, but she was also born with a stubborn drive to prove herself. If someone challenged her to do five push-ups, she'd do 10. If someone said Simone could not perform a skill, it only made her want to do the skill better than anyone else. Simone admits her stubbornness is her best and worst quality. But she says it became "mostly a good thing" when she got into gymnastics.

And there's one more reason Simone excels in gymnastics. She has an abundance of energy, what she calls a "special superpower!" Simone believes her superpower is why she can fly almost 10 feet into the air during her tumbling passes, high enough to leap over a dinosaur. For as long as she can remember, people have wondered: *Who on earth has so much energy?*

Simone Arianne Biles came into this world on March 14, 1997 with everything she needed to achieve gymnastic greatness: the perfect body, a strong drive, and a superpower! But Simone did not possess the one thing she needed most of all: loving, supportive parents... until Hampaw and Hamma rescued her from foster care.

Chapter 2

"Hamma! Can I Play on That?"

Before Simone moved in with her foster family, she and her siblings (brother and sisters) lived with their pretty, young mother, Shanon, in Columbus, Ohio. Simone did not know her father because he was never around.

Without help from Simone's father, Shanon struggled to feed and care for her children. When she had no money to buy baby milk, she stole 10 cases of it and got into big trouble. Things got even worse for Shanon when the neighbors noticed her children playing alone in the street while she was away. Concerned for their safety and well-being, they called a social worker. Social workers sometimes place children with other families until it is safe for them to return to their homes.

Simone doesn't remember much about living with Shanon before the social worker took her away when she was three. But she does remember not liking the cat hanging around her house. Simone remembers the cat always having food, and she didn't.

In *Simone vs. Herself,* Simone admitted: "I think that's where it stemmed, why I don't like cats. This freaking street cat... she [Shanon] always fed it, but she never fed us." Sometimes, all Simone had to eat was cereal with water poured over it.

The day the social worker came was the last day Simone watched the street cat eat while she was hungry. On that day, Simone recalls sitting on the front steps of Shanon's house with Tevin, her older sister Ashley, and baby sister Adria. She remembers the social worker, a woman Simone describes as a "warm-hearted African-American," saying: "We're placing you kids in foster care."

"It's just for a little while, so Shanon can try to get better," the social worker assured the frightened children. Although Simone was only three, she clearly understood what "placing you kids in foster care" meant: she was going away to live with another family.

Simone's next memory is getting into the back seat of the social worker's car. She recalls not saying a word during the ride. Neither did Tevin or 10-year-old Ashley, who held her baby sister, Adria, in her lap. Simone was frightened because she did not know if she would like her new family.

But when Miss Doris served a delicious dinner the first night, Simone decided her new family was much better than her old one—they had food! Running around with the other kids and Teddy, the dog, sealed the deal. And best of all, her foster parents did not have a cat!

However, accepting their new living situation was not as easy for Tevin and Ashley. They were older and had fond memories of Shanon that Simone did not have. And even though Miss Doris, whom Simone describes as a "softie," and Mr. Leo were very kind to them, Tevin and Ashley missed their mom and wanted to go home.

Simone did not want to go home. She was much happier living with her foster parents and their cookie jar. The day she spied it on the kitchen counter high above her reach full of cookies and candy, Miss Doris caught Simone trying to open it and cried out, "Simone, don't ever climb up here again!" Simone was not frightened by the scolding. It was a small price to pay for the lollipop Miss Doris placed in Simone's hand as she lowered the clever little girl to the floor.

While living in her foster home, Simone learned there were three areas where she was not allowed: the kitchen counter, the boys' bedroom, and the trampoline. Simone begged Miss Doris and Mr. Leo to let her bounce on it, but every time she asked, they said, "No." Their refusal confused Simone because Miss Doris and Mr. Leo allowed their biological children to jump on the trampoline. Simone did not know a foster parent's number one job is to protect their foster children until it is safe for them to return home. Miss Doris and Mr. Leo did not want Simone to get hurt.

Simone was not interested in any of that safety stuff. She just wanted to play with the other kids and did not understand why she couldn't. Simone was sure she could flip and jump higher than Miss Doris and Mr. Leo's kids. In a few short months, Simone would prove she was right—Hampaw Biles was coming to get her, and he had a trampoline in his backyard!

Simone could not pronounce her Gs when she began calling her grandparents "Hamma" and "Hampaw" during their visits with her in Ohio. Simone stopped whatever she was doing when the tall man with medium-brown skin and salt-and-pepper whiskers walked through the door. Hampaw was the person Simone always wanted to see.

Hampaw (Ron Biles) was Simone's grandfather and Shanon's father. He did not like his grandkids being "scattered to strangers" in foster care; he wanted to bring them to his home in Texas. However, the social worker and Ron's current wife, Nellie (Hamma), needed to agree to let him do it.

Taking in four young ones would dramatically change Nellie's life. She needed time to think about what her husband had asked her to do. Nellie looked forward to her teenage sons, Ron

II and Adam, being old enough to live on their own so she and Ron could take long trips together. If Nellie agreed to move the grandchildren in with her, she would have to put her plans on hold. Little did Nellie know she and Ron would travel all over the world one day because of Simone.

While trying to make up her mind, Nellie recalled her childhood in Belize, a tropical country on the Caribbean coast of Central America. The woman with pale brown skin and soft brown hair remembered living with cousins, aunts, and uncles in need of a place to stay during bad times. Nellie wondered if she could open her heart and her home to her needy family in the same selfless way her mother and father had opened theirs.

Nellie did not know what to do until she bumped into a stranger she called her guardian angel. The guardian angel said, "The Lord doesn't make any mistakes, and he never gives you more than you can handle." Nellie believed the angel was delivering a message from God to assure her everything would be okay if she agreed to bring the children into her home.

With God's guidance and the social worker's permission, Hampaw was soon on his way to get his grandchildren.

"Grandpa's here," Tevin whispered as he spied his grandfather on Miss Doris and Mr. Leo's front steps. Grandpa Biles had arrived with a big announcement: all four grandkids were going home with him the next day. Tevin and Ashley did not want to leave Ohio and whimpered most of the way to Texas. But Simone did not cry. She was happy to go with Hampaw in the big airplane and could not stop smiling at him.

"Oh no, little miss Simone, you're not going to steal my heart," Ron teased his granddaughter during the flight. But "little miss Simone" had already stolen Ron's heart the day he chose her name. Ron did not know anyone named Simone until he was a teenager and began listening to Nina Simone's records. Ron liked Nina's music and the sound of her last name. One look at his baby granddaughter was all it took to know *Simone* was the perfect name for her. It comforts Simone to know Grandpa Biles was with her "right from the start," watching over her and leading the way.

The day Hampaw led the way to her new home was one of the happiest days of young Simone's life. She still recalls the drive from the airport to Spring, Texas, 25 miles north of Houston. She remembers the beads in her braids swinging around her face as she bolted out of the car and ran into her grandparents' house.

Once inside, Simone's big brown eyes took it all in: the shiny, bright floors, the large eat-in kitchen, and the wide stairway to her bedroom. Simone had never seen a house so big or so beautiful. And she had never seen so many toys, books, and clothes just for her.

But her attention quickly moved from the toys inside the house to the BIG toy outside. "Hamma! Hamma! Can I play on that?" shouted Simone as she pointed to the window in her bedroom. Hamma did not know what Simone was talking about, but Hamma's teenage son, Adam, did: "The trampoline? Sure! Want to go jump on it right now?"

Simone's mouth fell open, and her eyes grew wide. Was she hearing what she thought she did? Instead of "NO," Simone heard these three words: *sure*, *jump*, and *now*!

Simone could not get down the stairs and out the door fast enough to the trampoline, waiting just for her! "For what seemed like hours, I bounced and twirled and flipped and somersaulted, my beaded braids flying up into the sky again and again, as if they could touch heaven," Simone recalled in her autobiography, *Courage to Soar*.

Living in Spring felt like heaven to three-year-old Simone. She cherished everything about her new life. But, there was one small problem: Hamma insisted Simone eat meat and vegetables each night before leaving the table. Hamma did not know Simone disliked how meat felt in her mouth and how vegetables tasted.

The same strong-willed child who did not obey Miss Doris when she said she must sleep in her bed did not obey Hamma either. With thoughts of gooey, cheesy pizza in her head, Simone drifted off to sleep at the table many nights, refusing to eat her meal. But one evening, Simone excused herself and left a clean plate behind. It was as if she waved a magic wand, and the meat and vegetables disappeared. Had Simone given in to her grandmother's demands to eat all her food? Or was something else going on during dinner every night?

Simone and Hamma were getting along really well until the day Hamma cleaned Simone's booster seat and found a big surprise underneath it. And it was no magic wand! It was gunky old carrots, potatoes, meatloaf, and chicken nuggets Simone had stuffed in a hollow space under her seat.

"Simone, you're going to eat every bite of this!" Hamma demanded. Of course, Hamma did not make Simone eat that smelly old food. She was only trying to make Simone understand that hiding her dinner in her booster chair was wasteful.

Hamma had to find a way to get Simone to eat something besides her favorite foods, pizza and pasta. So, she and Simone compromised (each gave in a little). Simone agreed to eat her food if Hamma ground it up and put it over noodles. The standoff between Hamma and Simone was finally over.

Simone and her grandmother were not constantly battling each other in those early days. They often spent tender moments together while Hamma washed, combed, and braided Simone's hair. The attention Hamma gave Simone made her feel special. By age six, Simone had learned some news to make her feel special for the rest of her life.

Houston
International Airport

Chapter 3

"Finally and Forever Home"

Simone could not imagine life anywhere other than with her grandparents. She loved them and they loved her. She never wanted to leave them. But after about a year, the social worker sent her, Tevin, Ashley, and Adria back to their foster parents, Miss Doris and Mr. Leo.

Bouncing from one home to another was not working out for Simone. She was becoming less talkative and shy, and she missed her grandparents. She and her brother and sisters needed a forever home. Since their mother, Shanon, never did "get better," the social worker placed Simone and Adria permanently with their grandparents in Texas. The social worker placed Tevin and Ashley with their aunt in Ohio.

On Christmas Eve, 2002, five-year-old Simone and three-year-old Adria boarded a plane from Ohio for one more trip to Texas with Hampaw, this time to stay forever. Simone remembers thinking that being back in Spring felt like her own "Christmas miracle."

It wasn't long before Simone, Adria, Hamma, and Hampaw began to feel like a family. No one was ever going to break them up again. "They were mine now, and I was theirs," Simone shared in her autobiography.

One unforgettable day, instead of stepping into her favorite overalls and running to the trampoline, Simone slipped into what she called a "very girly dress." It was blue, her favorite color. The same day, Nellie helped Adria into her favorite pink dress and clipped matching barrettes into the girls' hair. Ron traded his casual clothes for his best work clothes, and Nellie put on her expensive jewelry. The new family had an appointment with a judge at the courthouse, and Nellie wanted them to look their best.

Because Simone was only six and Adria was only four, they were not old enough to understand why they were in a judge's office. But they were old enough to know the papers he shuffled must have been very important, since they wore pretty dresses to watch him sign them.

Later that evening, before bedtime, Simone noticed a different tone in her grandmother's voice when she shared some news: "You know, girls, we adopted you both today." Suddenly, the trip to the courthouse made sense, and Simone asked, "Does that mean I can call you Mom and Dad?"

"It's up to you. Call us whatever you want. Now go to bed," Nellie replied, with one hand lovingly touching Simone's cheek and the other stroking Adria's hair. That night, to be sure her grandparents would answer to their new names, Simone called out first to Nellie: "Mom?" Then to Ron: "Dad?" When they both answered, Simone knew she and Adria were "finally and forever home."

When they adopted Simone and Adria, Nellie was a traveling nurse and Ron was an air traffic controller (someone who ensures airplanes do not get too close in the air). While they were away at work, Simone and Adria attended a "Kids R Kids" daycare, where their new big brother Adam was a part-time teacher.

Little Simone squealed with excitement the days the teachers passed out the "Kids R Kids" blue T-shirts. When the blue shirts came out, it was field trip day! Simone especially liked the trips outside, where she could do backflips and somersaults.

One summer day, Simone and the other kids put on their "Kids R Kids" shirts and prepared to spend the day on a farm in the country. But Simone sensed something was wrong when she noticed the worried look on Adam's face as he looked out the window.

The pouring rain had washed away the outing to the farm. The teachers would have to come up with another plan for the day. Adam suggested the kids visit Bannon's Gymnastix down the street. He believed his bouncy, energetic kid sister would like tumbling and flipping in a gym way more than tiptoeing through a museum.

When they entered the gym and Simone took off running, Adam knew his idea to go to Bannon's was a good one. He was not surprised to see his sister imitate the older gymnasts as she dashed from the low beam to the low bars and then to the kiddie springboard. But he was shocked when Simone did a backflip with a slight twist on the layout and landed on her feet. And so was Ronnie, one of the coaches at the gym.

"Is this your daughter?" Ronnie asked Adam as she observed Simone jumping and flipping off the low bars. "Whoa! I'm no one's dad. This is my little sister," replied Adam. He was only 18 years old.

Ronnie wondered if Simone had taken classes at another gym. When Adam told Ronnie Simone had never taken a gymnastics class, Ronnie decided it was time she did.

Within a few days, Nellie enrolled Simone and Adria in recreational gymnastics classes two times a week at Bannon's. During Simone's first class, Ronnie asked one of the other coaches, who happened to be her daughter, Aimee, to observe the new kid in the gym. Two weeks passed before the pretty blonde coach finally took a look at Simone.

Aimee recalled that day: "I saw this teeny, petite thing with rippling muscles who was just full of energy and couldn't stay still." Aimee could not keep her eyes off the bundle of energy in the gym doing moves six-year-olds shouldn't be able to do. One day, Simone did a seat drop, a bounce from a sitting position back to her feet as if she were on a trampoline. Aimee thought, *Okay, that's not normal.*

Simone and Adria soon joined Bannon's Jet Star team and entered the USA Gymnastics (USAG) Junior Olympic (JO) program. In the JO program, gymnasts can advance through 10 skill levels and compete in district, state, regional, and national competitions.

Both Simone and Adria were natural gymnasts and easily advanced through the lower skill levels to become popular "Jet Stars." Adria was never as enthusiastic about gymnastics as Simone was. She dropped out a month after making the "Jet Star" team to become a Girl Scout Brownie.

Young Simone had no idea how good she was at gymnastics. But Simone's coach, Aimee, did. She recognized Simone's extraordinary ability to sense where she was in the air as she tumbled. Even at six years old, Simone could bring her feet down at the exact moment to land upright. One day at age seven, Simone wowed her coaches: She imitated older gymnasts and did a back tuck (a backward flip from a standing position with the knees "tucked" to the chest) and landed it on the gym floor. And she blew them away when she did it again on the floor beam and did not fall off it.

Simone wasn't always at the gym during those first few years in Spring. She and Adria spent most days in the cul-de-sac (a dead-end street with a rounded end) in front of their house. Simone and Adria entertained themselves for hours in the cul-de-sac, riding their bikes and driving their toy cars with their baby dolls. Simone, in her Hummer, and Adria, in her Barbi Jeep, acted like mothers returning from work, checking their mail at the mailboxes on their street.

When Adria reached her sister's height, neither she nor Simone fit into their toy cars anymore. One summer, the adorable look-alike sisters with the movie star smiles discovered something as fun as driving cars. Along with their neighborhood friends, Marissa and Becca, Simone and Adria danced into a fantasy world and became Cheetah Girls. The Cheetah Girls were characters in a TV musical about four high school friends in a rock band. In the land of make-believe, Simone was Galleria, Marissa was Chanel, Becca was Dorinda, and Adria was Aquanette.

The make-believe Cheetahs were not only talented singers, they were also builders. When they agreed the band needed a suitable place to practice, the

Cheetahs constructed a clubhouse in Becca's backyard with sheets of leftover plywood. It was barely big enough for them to huddle together inside. The opening was so narrow the girls had to crawl through it. And the flimsy structure could have easily come tumbling down any minute. As it turned out, the only thing tumbling down was a spider that landed on Marissa's head!

After the spider ran them out of the "Cheetah Girls Clubhouse," the Texas Cheetahs never met at the clubhouse again. Simone's days of pretending to be a superstar were over. She was becoming a real superstar in the gym!

Simone was doing so well that some of the coaches at Bannon's feared she was competing too much and could burn out. But Aimee argued Simone was having fun and they should allow her to compete as much as she wanted. Doing gymnastics felt like flying to Simone, and Simone loved nothing more than flying. After all, she had been doing it since she was a tiny tot, when she soared off the backyard swing or skyrocketed off the trampoline. There was no way she was going to stop flying now.

Chapter 4

"You're That Good!"

By the time Simone was 11, she competed in district and state gymnastic competitions in Texas and was eligible for regional meets. In her region, Region 3, Simone would compete against gymnasts from Texas and six other states. If she could earn a score of 34 or higher at the upcoming Region 3 Championships, she would qualify for the level 9 Western Championships.

Qualifying for Westerns wasn't the only reason Simone wanted to receive a high score at regionals. It was something else: her dad's promise to get her a dog. Year after year, Simone and Adria asked for a new puppy, but Poppa Biles did not think his daughters were old enough to care for a dog.

Poppa Biles was certain Simone and Adria would stop begging for a puppy the Christmas he squeezed two super-size stuffed ones under the tree. But they did not. Realizing his persistent daughters were not going to give up, Poppa Biles made a deal with Simone: "Okay, Simone, I'll tell you what. You qualify for Westerns this year, and you'll get your dog."

In *Courage to Soar,* Simone explained her motivation to hit all her routines at the Regional Championships came from her dad's promise. She placed first on the floor exercise and second in the all-around competition.

Simone had done her best, but would it be good enough to get the dog? Would her final score be at least 34 and qualify her for the Westerns? There was no doubt Simone had indeed scored high enough when she heard Adria screaming from the stands: "We're getting a dog! We're getting a dog!"

Simone took her 38.100 score straight to the nearby German shepherd farm to get her prize. But there were so many puppies on the farm. How would

Simone ever choose? They were all adorable. The small brown-and-black girl puppy scooting around in its pen stood out among all the others. The energetic pup was a lot like Simone.

Simone wasn't sure if the playful little doggie was the one she wanted until she held it, and it began licking her face. After all those puppy kisses, Simone made her decision. The precious pup in Simone's arms was going home with her! Simone reminded her family she had "won" the pup and the right to name her. Maggie Elena Biles, the German shepherd, lived the rest of her life with Simone and her family.

In a 2017 Instagram post, Simone wrote about Maggie:

"You were my first dog, the dog I begged and begged my parents to get. So you were my present when I made level nine Westerns, I got to name you (Maggie). We grew up together. The craziest most unbothered dog!! You were amazing. Have fun in Doggie Heaven, Maggie Maggie. I love you!"

Maggie joined the Biles family the summer before Simone started seventh grade at Strack Intermediate. Simone felt like she was passing time at Strack because she was moving to a new house and going to another school soon. Although she was excited about the bigger house with the saltwater pool, leaving her old friends at Strack and missing next year's eighth-grade dance made Simone sad.

Simone had reached level 10 in gymnastics. At level 10 and then at the elite level (the highest level), gymnasts must add more hours to their weekly training schedule. However, because the new house was 45 minutes from Bannon's, Simone would have to spend almost two hours on the road and not in the gym. Aimee and Nellie struggled to find a way around the problem.

The solution was there all along: Simone would attend the private school across the street from Bannon's and walk back and forth to the gym from school—problem solved! But all was not well at the new school. Simone's teacher never pronounced her name correctly.

He called her "Somalia" the entire time she was in his class.

Poor "Somalia's" eighth-grade year was not so great either. Most of the kids at her new school either had behavior problems or learning challenges. A boy in Simone's class with severe behavior problems could have badly injured her when he tried to stab her hand. Thankfully, his aim was off, and he missed.

Afraid the scary kid might try again, Simone bolted out of the classroom with him close behind, his pocketknife still in his hand. But he was no match for a Level 10 gymnast. Simone easily outran him and jumped over a gate to safety in the school office...or so she thought.

The lady at the front desk did not believe Simone when she told her what had happened. But Simone's parents did. After a teacher-parent conference, the teachers agreed to separate Simone from the out-of-control kid for the rest of the year.

The only good thing about the private school was its location. Simone arrived at Bannon's at seven in the morning each school day, practiced for two hours, and then walked to school. After her classes, she walked back to the gym to work out for another two hours.

With all the extra hours of practice, Simone's gymnastic skills dramatically improved. At the Houston National

Invitational, her first Level 10 meet, 13-year-old Simone placed first on vault and floor and third all-around. After Simone performed so well at the Houston National, Aimee believed Simone was ready to attend a developmental camp at Karolyi's training center (the Ranch) in Huntsville, Texas. Hoping for an invitation, Aimee sent a video of Simone's routines to Martha Karolyi, the USA Gymnastics coordinator.

Aimee did not expect this response from Martha: "This kid has no bars. I can't let her come to camp. She can tumble great, but that's it." Until Simone improved her bar routines, Martha was not interested in working with her.

Simone was the kid with "no bars" because she did not like the bars and avoided them. She preferred floor, vault, and beam, where she could use every bit of her superpower to fly through the air without a bar snatching her back down.

Nellie wondered if Simone's bar routines would improve if she had a new coach in another gymnastics program. But Simone preferred to stay with Aimee and did not want to go to another gym. Simone trusted Aimee; she felt like a member of Simone's family. When Aimee offered to bring in another coach if Simone did not improve, Nellie agreed to allow Simone to continue training at Bannon's. Keeping Simone and Aimee together was the right decision.

Aimee's encouragement helped Simone more than anything: "Okay, Simone, go out there and enjoy yourself. Do your best and don't worry about the rest." And that's what Simone did, winning fourth all-around and first on vault at the Region 3 Championships. At Nationals in Dallas, Simone placed first on the floor and third all-around. Thirteen-year-old Simone Biles ended the 2010 season as the US Challenge Pre-Elite All-Around Champion.

Aimee never forgot the day seven-year-old Simone landed a back tuck on the low beam at Bannon's. That was the day she realized Simone had what it took to make it to the Nationals, Worlds, and maybe even the Olympics.

Aimee believed it then and still believed it six years later. She wanted Martha Karolyi to believe it, too.

So, once again, Aimee sent recordings of Simone's routines to Martha. As Martha viewed the videos, she noticed much improvement in Simone. However, Martha wondered if it was too late to turn Simone into a world-class athlete.

Martha preferred to start training girls much younger than Simone. Before Martha came to the United States, she lived in Romania and coached Olympic champions with her husband, Bela. She and Bela began working with the 1976 Olympic Champion, Nadia Comaneci, when Nadi was seven.

Martha must have seen something she liked in the *old* kid this time. Was it Simone's improved bar routines? Was it Simone's fierce determination and drive? Or was it Simone's recent win at the Gliders National Elite Qualifier? Simone never learned why Martha changed her mind and invited her to a developmental camp at the Ranch. The reason was unimportant to her. What mattered most to Simone was that she was going!

They called the Karolyi training center the "Ranch" because it rested on 2,000 acres in a national forest. The Ranch had cabins for as many as three hundred athletes and coaches. Around a large lake were three gyms, a dining hall, and a medical clinic.

During Simone's five days at the Ranch, she worked on her gymnastic skills from eight in the morning until seven at night, breaking to eat and rest for three hours. On the first day at the Ranch, Simone discovered Martha would think she was not committed to her sport if she cried or laughed during workouts. Simone held back tears on the days she was so exhausted she wondered if she could keep going. She did not want to disappoint Martha.

Simone recalls lining up with the other girls at the end of practice one day and hearing Martha say in her Eastern European accent, "We strive for perfection here. If that's not your goal, then you're in the wrong place."

Simone felt she was in the wrong place the first few days. She missed laughing and acting silly with her friends while she practiced. But Simone understood she was exactly where she needed to be to become a champion. Simone had to accept that gymnastics was not always fun and games. Sometimes, it was work!

A few weeks after Simone left the Ranch, she found herself there again for the American Classic Gymnastics competition. Simone won first on the vault and first on the balance beam because of Martha's intense training and results-oriented approach. Her 53.650 score was high enough to qualify for the 2011 Visa National Championship, or as Simone called it, her "golden ticket." A good Nationals performance guaranteed Simone a spot on the next artistic USA women's junior team. But Simone would have to add new "dream skills" to her routines to cash in that ticket.

Simone wrote in her journal about the "dream skills" she learned: "I just got some new skills on beam, an aerial [which is a cartwheel with no hands], and a round-off double into the pit." She also noted she was working on the Tkatchev, a hard-to-do release-and-catch move on the uneven bars named after the Russian gymnast Alexander Tkatchev. She did not write in her journal she had been trying to do the

Tkatchev (pronounced "Te-catch-ev") for a year and couldn't *catch* it.

To make the situation even more problematic, one day, while practicing the Tkatchev, Simone did not release the high bar at the right time. Instead of flying backward over the bar and grabbing it on the other side, Simone missed it and flew into the air, landing with a thud on the mat. "What are you doing? You can't do that! You have to follow through with the skill or you'll get injured," one of the coaches yelled.

The mishap on the bars did not hurt Simone's body, but it caused something just as harmful as an injury. It made Simone fear the Tkatchev. Simone may have never attempted to do the Tkatchev again if she had not been stubborn. The 14-year-old gymnast refused to let the scary skill keep her from making the women's junior national team.

The battle between Simone and the Tkatchev seemed to last forever. Simone's timing was off. She would either grab the bar too early and slam into it or release too late and crash onto the mat below. Simone could not defeat her opponent. The Tkatchev won every time.

"Aimee, I'm never going to get it!" Simone cried out from her tear-stained face during one of the 45-minute bar rotations. In her book, Simone explained she would "miss, cry, miss, cry, miss, cry" until she repeated these words over and over in her head: *I'm going to do it this time!*

So, at the end of one of the practice sessions, Simone mounted the uneven bars for one more dual with her foe, the Tkatchev. And to her amazement, Simone finally caught the high bar and completed the skill. The war of Biles vs. the Tkatchev was over! Simone won!

With the Tkatchev conquered, Simone was more prepared for the Visa National Championships. She hoped to be one of the 13 chosen for the USA junior team. Simone may have made the team if she had taken her other rival, the Amanar, with her.

An Amanar is a back handspring off the vaulting table with a layout and two and a half twists named after the Romanian gymnast Simona Amanar. It is one of the most difficult vaults to do in gymnastics because it requires high power and precision.

But Simone did not attempt the Amanar at Nationals. She listened to her body when it said: *We're not ready to do the Amanar unless you want to leave the arena on a stretcher.* Without the Amanar, Simone placed 14th and did not win a spot on the 13-member junior team.

Coming so close to making the national team brought Simone to her knees, and she cried at the hotel after the competition. Her dad's pats on her shoulder and her mom's rubs on her back comforted Simone but did not stop the tears. But when the phone rang, the sobbing suddenly stopped.

It was Simone's brother Ron with a tear-drying pep talk for his sister: "Because you know what, Simone, you can use this as motivation to go into the gym and train even harder. Coming in at number 14 means you're almost there!" Ron continued, "Maybe it's not your time yet, but trust me, your day will come because you're that good."

Ron spoke the truth when he said Simone was "that good!" Good enough to go all the way to the Olympics!

Rio 2016

Chapter 5

"That Could Be You, Simone!"

After failing to make the USA junior team, Simone did what she had always done. She picked herself up and got to work. If Simone was going to make next year's team, she needed to increase the difficulty of her routines and earn a higher score at Nationals. That meant she would have to spend more time in the gym. Simone was already training 25 to 30 hours a week, but that was not enough. She needed five more hours to perfect her skills.

As the time to enter the ninth grade grew near, 14-year-old Simone faced one of the most crucial decisions of her life: attend high school or be homeschooled. Going to high school full-time and working 35 hours a week in the gym is nearly impossible, so most elite athletes choose homeschooling.

Simone's two worlds were colliding, crushing her between them. Simone wanted to live in both of them—the high school world and the gymnastics world. She struggled to decide what she wanted to do more: pal around with her teenage friends at school or travel worldwide with gymnasts she had admired for years. Simone accepted she would have to give up something no matter what she chose.

Simone pleaded with her parents to decide for her, but only Simone could choose. After all, the choice affected her, not them. For weeks, Simone remained uncertain until she remembered something her dad had said years ago: "Simone, never squander what God has given you."

God had given Simone the body, the drive, and the talent to be a world-class athlete. She believed if she used these gifts wisely and put in enough time in the gym, she could make the national team and someday even make it to the Olympics.

When Simone was 11, she wrote in her diary: "I want to go the farthest I can." Simone's feelings had not changed three years later. She still wanted to go "the farthest" she could. But the only way to get there was through homeschooling.

For Simone, homeschooling was more like *gymschooling*. Her teacher met her at Bannon's three days a week to teach her the same lessons taught in the public high school. Simone spent the other two days doing her schoolwork alone at the gym.

All was going well with Simone's schoolwork, but not so well with her gymnastics. Simone was tired of her coaches telling her what to do, so she began talking back to them under her breath. Simone believes her rebellious attitude had less to do with gymnastics and more to do with her resentment at having to give up public school.

Aimee had worked for years with sassy, whiney 13- and 14-year-old girls going through what she labeled their "bratty period." Aimee was more than capable of dealing with them and did a little mumbling under her breath, too: *Go ahead, have your attitude, but do the work.* Teenage girls did not scare her.

With the start of the 2012 competitive season in January, Simone's bratty period was over. She had a new attitude and a new skill—the Amanar! Simone concluded back in 2011 that the only way to make it on the national team was to master the Amanar. For the entire 2012 season, Simone and her new best friend, the Amanar, placed first on vault in every meet. With her first-place vault performance at the 2012 Visa National Championships, Simone won the big prize—she made the junior women's national team!

The year Simone made the junior team was a big year for women's gymnastics. It was an Olympic year! Simone, her coaches, and fellow gymnasts gathered at Bannon's in front of a big screen to watch the five-member USA Olympic team, the "Fierce Five," win the 2012 team gold medal. As the purple ribbon with the gold medal attached slipped over each girl's head, Simone wondered: *What would it feel like to stand on the Olympic podium with my teammates someday?*

Startled from her daydream, Simone heard one of the girls in the gym shout: "That could be you, Simone!" Followed by shouts of: "2016 Olympics, Simone! You can do it! That will be you!" At that moment, Simone began believing she could make it to the Olympics. And she prayed to God to help her get there.

The following January in 2013, while at Nationals Camp on the Ranch, Simone received some big news from Martha: "The two girls who will be competing at the American Cup this year are Katelyn Ohashi and Simone Biles." Simone was thrilled Martha selected her good buddy, Katelyn, the other half of "Double-Trouble," to go with her to the American Cup.

But Simone's enthusiasm switched to panic on the first day of the competition when her stomach twisted into painful knots. The pressure of having television cameras, a large crowd, and Martha watching her compete caused Simone's stomach to hurt. Simone wondered if she was well enough to compete.

Martha explained to Simone that having bellyaches before competitions was normal. Martha assured Simone that her nerves were causing them and that she was not physically ill. With

Martha's comforting words, Simone relaxed and performed well enough to place second despite a fall on the balance beam.

The fall at the American Cup would not be Simone's last one during a competition. Four months later, she flew off the high bar at the US Secret Classic and crashed onto the mat. Simone's old enemy, the Tkatchev, took her down. Her beam routine was almost as bad. Simone swayed back and forth between skills, barely hanging onto the beam. Her floor routine was even worse. On her last tumbling pass, she landed on her ankles, fell forward onto her knees, and almost smashed her face into the mat.

When Aimee noticed Simone limping, she pulled her away from the other girls and said, "Simone, you're not mentally in the game. And you're in danger of badly injuring yourself. I'm sorry, but I'm not going to let you do that. You're out. That's it."

No one expected Simone to perform so poorly and leave the competition. Some said Simone "crashed" because she was "fat." However, her weight had not changed since she won two gold medals in Europe a few months earlier.

But the truth is, the pressure to compete without mistakes was negatively affecting Simone's performance. Talking with her sports psychologist always made Simone feel better. He advised her to stop worrying about what everyone expected of her: "You never did that before, so you don't have to do it now. Don't change what has always worked for you, which is to go out there and just have fun."

Simone's psychologist reminded her if she was having fun, she was winning. And that's just what she did a few weeks later at the P&G National Championships. Simone was flying high again and having the time of her life. Not only did she win the gold medal to become the 2013 US National all-around champion, but she also won a spot on the US national senior team. Three weeks later, the USAG chose Simone to compete for the United States at the World Championships in Antwerp, Belgium.

As Simone packed her bags for the trip to Worlds, she selected six turtles from her figurine collection to take with her. The turtles reminded Simone to carry everyone's expectations of her lightly, the same way a turtle carries its shell. The lucky one with the ladybug on its back did not let Simone down. Simone won the gold and became the 2013 Artistic Gymnastics world champion!

And something else exciting happened at Worlds. Simone added a new move to her floor routine—a double flip in the layout position with a half twist out. Since Simone created the combination and executed it flawlessly at the World Championships, it officially became known as the Biles.

Simone was 16 when she became a world champion. At 17, she earned another all-around World title. The year after Simone's second win at Worlds, people began to wonder if she could win a third time. Chants of *three-peat, three-peat, three-peat* blew up Simone's Twitter feed. It was certainly possible. Simone had not lost a meet since winning Nationals in 2013. She was a three-time US national champion and two-time world champion going to the World Championships in Glasgow, Scotland.

Simone felt what she described as an "unbelievable amount of pressure" going to Worlds because everyone expected her to win again. Letting off steam by laughing and joking about the silliest things with her roommate calmed Simone's nerves. And like the true champion she was, Simone won the all-around gold medal and gave her fans what they wanted: the three-peat!

Simone's win at Worlds happened at the ideal time. The gymnastics training center her parents had been building for two years was finally complete. Everything was in place: the mats, the foam pit, and all the equipment. The World Champions Centre, WCC, needed one more addition: a world champion to walk through its doors. No problem! The owner's daughter was on her way with three World Championships gold medals!

Going through the WCC door was a breeze. However, selecting between two other open doors would be more challenging. Simone could either choose the door to college or the door to the Olympics. Simone's predicament felt like the one she was in four years earlier: choosing between high school or homeschooling.

Simone had dreams of joining a college gymnastics team and competing in the 2016 Olympics since she was 13.

Only five years later, both dreams were coming true. The University of California, Los Angeles (UCLA) invited Simone to join their gymnastics team. But at the same time, Simone was on track to compete at the 2016 Olympics in Rio de Janeiro, Brazil.

Once again, Simone had to make a life-changing decision. Should she spend a year sharpening her skills for the Olympics or be a freshman at UCLA competing with the women's gymnastics team? If Simone chose to enter UCLA, she could attend school football games and parties to make up for the ones she had missed during high school.

But if Simone chose the door to the Olympics, she could become an Olympic champion. And she could be a professional athlete and make money doing what she loved. Which door should she choose?

Chapter 6

"I Will Make You Proud"

Simone chose the door to the 2016 Olympics! The college dream could wait, but the Olympic dream could not. No one could be certain if Simone would still be at the Olympic level in four years at the 2020 Olympics. She was at the top of her game now.

Dozens of companies stood in line with contracts after Simone put her college dream aside and became a professional athlete. Simone had so many offers she had to hire an agent to help her decide which brands to choose. Proctor and Gamble, United Airlines, Hershey's, Core Power sports drinks, and Nike were Simone's favorites. Kellogg's Special K cereal star was a natural promoter of laundry detergent, airline travel, chocolate bars, and power drinks. Simone's Nike commercial encouraged people to "just be the best."

The months leading up to the 2016 Olympics were busy ones for Simone. In addition to earning thousands of dollars making commercials, the three-time world champion continued her winning streak. First was her all-around gold medal win at the Pacific

Rim Championships in April, followed by another win at the P&G National Championships in June. Then came a first-place finish at the Olympic Trials two weeks later.

Simone wrote in *Courage to Soar* that her "Olympic dream had never been about winning—it was about *going*," and having her name called as a member of the team. Simone's dream came true the day Martha announced the names of the five girls on the 2016 Olympic women's team: Gabby Douglas, Laurie Hernandez, Madison Kocian, Aly Raisman, and SIMONE BILES!

Simone and the other girls would be Martha's "final" Olympic team to coach because she was retiring soon.

To honor Martha, the new USA team chose to call themselves the "Final Five." They wanted to win Martha one more gold medal. But to get it, the Final Five would have to spend 10 long days training at the Ranch to fine-tune their skills.

Simone was nervous about spending almost two weeks at the Ranch. She remembered how exhausting only five days were. As she and Aimee made the familiar drive down the winding road to meet Martha, Simone grabbed her throat and cried out, "Aimee, we're all going to die! Save us, please!"

"Yes, you will die. And all your hair will fall out too," Aimee replied. Simone and Aimee had been together enough time to know joking around calmed their nerves during stressful times.

Near the end of their training, Simone and her teammates looked forward to some much-needed downtime with their families at the open house. It would be Simone's last time to see her mom, dad, and Adria before they reunited at the Olympics.

Before Nellie kissed her daughter goodbye at the family gathering on the Ranch, she pulled her aside for one last piece of motherly advice. Nellie encouraged her daughter to "get clear on what she wanted to accomplish in Rio" and to write it down. Simone had already accomplished what she had set out to do. Was there something else that meant just as much to her as making the team and going to the Olympics?

Simone replayed her last conversation with her mother in her head for days. Nellie's loving, gentle voice had guided and comforted Simone for most of her life. Hearing it at the open house reminded Simone of how thankful she was to have been adopted and loved by her grandparents. It also reminded Simone that there was something more important to her than the Olympics.

The day before flying to Rio, Simone grabbed a notebook and wrote a short letter to her parents. In the letter, Simone made a promise to Ron and Nellie, making her Olympic intentions quite clear.

To be sure her parents read the letter, Simone slipped the notebook between two of her sweaty leotards and sent it home with the rest of her dirty laundry.

Two weeks later, on Sunday, August 7, 2016, the most decorated female in gymnastic sports history made her Olympic debut in Rio de Janeiro, Brazil. After her first rotation in the qualification rounds, 19-year-old Simone Biles heard these words from her teammate Laurie: "Hey, Simone, guess what? You are now officially an Olympian." A lifetime of sacrifices, discipline, and hard work had led Simone to this moment. And she was ready!

Four years earlier, Simone wondered what standing with her teammates on an Olympic podium would feel like. Two days after the qualification rounds, she had her answer. The USA women's team won the gold medal! Standing with the Final Five on the podium, Simone thought, *Wow, we did it. How long have I dreamed about this?* Simone felt happiness not only for herself but also for the other girls on the team, for Martha and Aimee, and for her parents, Ron and Nellie Biles.

Simone's journey to gymnastic greatness may have never begun if her grandparents had not given her what she describes as a "second shot at life." She is unsure if she would have been in gymnastics without their financial and emotional support.

In an interview with *USA Today,* Simone shared how she felt about being adopted by her grandparents: "It could have just been so different, and it's hard to think what my life could have been because it's not," Biles said. "So I'm just very grateful for the opportunity and to be adopted by family and have a good head on my shoulders, but also have that guidance. And for them to take such a leap of faith."

Ron and Nellie had been with Simone every step of the way on her journey to the Olympics, and they were with her on August 11, 2016. That was the day Nellie yelled one more time, "You've got this, Simone." That was the day Ron and Nellie Biles witnessed their daughter,

Simone Biles, win the all-around gold medal and become an Olympic champion. And that was the day Simone kept the promise written in the notebook she'd sent home with her laundry.

Hi Mom and Dad,

I love you all.

See you soon in Rio.

I will make you proud.

Love, Simone. Kisses

Bibliography

Armour, Nancy. "How Simone Biles Went from Foster Care to Olympic Great." *USA Today*, July 23, 2021. https://www.usatoday.com/story/sports/olympics/2021/07/23/2021-olympics-how-simone-biles-went-foster-care-olympic-great/7931081002/.

Armour, Nancy. "US Women's Gymnastics Team Claims Silver in Team Final After Simone Biles Withdraws at Tokyo Olympics." *USA Today*, July 27, 2021. https://www.usatoday.com/story/sports/olympics/2021/07/27/us-womens-gymnastics-silver-tokyo-olympics-simone-biles/5383082001/.

Biles, Simone. "A Dog Is a Part of Your Life." *Instagram*, March 17, 2017. https://www.instagram.com/p/BRvmoFNjP52/.

Biles, Simone, and Michelle Burford. *Courage to Soar. Zondervan*, 2016.

Bregman, Scott. "Simone Biles Back on Top with All-around Win at the 2023 U.S. Classic."

Olympics, August 5, 2023. https://olympics.com/en/news/simone-biles-win-2023-us-classic-core-hydration-results-paris-2024.

"Definition: Tkatchev." *Gymnastics Zone,* December 20, 2010. https://gymnasticszone.com/definition-tkatchev/.

Fieldstadt, Elisha. "Simone Biles Says Tokyo Bronze Means More than All Her Golds." *NBC News,* August 3, 2021. https://www.nbcnews.com/news/olympics/simone-biles-says-tokyo-bronze-means-more-all-her-golds-n1275804.

Gilmer, Marcus. "This Chart Shows Just How High Simone Biles Can Jump." *Mashable,* August 17, 2016. https://mashable.com/article/how-high-does-simone-biles-jump.

Gilroy, Rosie H. V. "The Amanar Vault Is A Winning Gymnastics Move." *Bustle,* August 4, 2016. https://www.bustle.com/articles/176815-what-is-the-amanar-vault-theres-a-long-story-behind-this-famous-us-gymnastics-move.

Gunston, Jo. "Simone Biles: All Titles, Records and Medals-complete List." *Olympics,* October 8, 2023. https://olympics.com/en/news/simone-biles-all-titles-records-medals-complete-list.

Hirsch, Chelsea. "Inside Gymnast Simone Biles' Tragic Early Days: Bio Mom Arrested For Stealing Baby Formula." *RADAR Online,* August 11, 2016. https://radaronline.com/

exclusives/2016/08/simone-biles-tragic-childhood-biological-mom-arrested-stealing-baby-formula/.

Mullin, Eric, and Kelley Ekert. "Simone Biles Shares Videos to Explain 'Twisties,' Answers Questions on Instagram." *NBC Sports Boston*, July 30, 2021. https://www.nbcsportsboston.com/tokyo-olympics/simone-biles-shares-videos-to-explain-twisties-answers-questions-on-instagram/185651/.

Murphy, Colleen, and Stephanie Hartselle MD. "'Twisties': The Mental Block That Affected Simone Biles." *Health*, December 21, 2022. https://www.health.com/condition/mental-health-conditions/simone-biles-twisties-gymnastics.

"Nadia Comaneci." *Olympics*. https://olympics.com/en/athletes/nadia-comaneci.

Park, Alice. "Simone Biles Returns to the Tokyo Olympics—With a Big Statement." *Time*, August 3, 2021. https://time.com/6086691/biles-returns-tokyo-olympics-bronze/.

Ross, Ashley. "The Couple That Changed Gymnastics: 3 Decades of Karolyi Highlights." *Time*, August 8, 2016. https://time.com/4434463/history-bela-martha-karolyi/.

Sanchez, Rosa. "Simone Biles Explains Competition Withdrawal at Olympics: 'My

Mind and Body Are Simply Not in Sync.'" *ABC News*, July 30, 2021. https://abcnews.go.com/Sports/simone-biles-explains-withdrawal-olympics-mind-body-simply/story?id=79157744.

"Simone Biles' Letter To Intimidated Teens." *Net-A-Porter*, November 23, 2016. https://www.net-a-porter.com/en-hk/porter/article-f2689e3c93882ed2/incredible-women/incredible-women/simone-biles-letter.

"Simone Biles Stumbles on Vault Before Pulling Out of Team Final." *YouTube*, uploaded by NBC Sports, July 27, 2021. https://www.youtube.com/watch?v=nO-vMUApyJQ.

Stump, Scott. "Simone Biles Says Physically She Feels 'good' but 'it Varies' Emotionally." *TODAY*, July 27, 2021. https://www.today.com/news/simone-biles-says-physically-she-feels-good-it-varies-emotionally-t226561.

"Who Am I?" *Simone Vs. Herself*, uploaded by Versus on Watch, June 29, 2021. https://www.facebook.com/vsonwatch/videos/2987343974844447/.

About the Author

Angela Gail Griffin, the award-winning author of *Women of the Wind,* has long been an admirer of successful, strong women. As a writer for the When They Were Kids series, Angela carries her young readers through the childhoods of famous women who were little girls with big dreams. Angela's books remind children that if they never stop doing what brings them joy, their dreams can come true, too.

Learn more about Angela and the women who inspired her to write her first book at www.womenofthewind.com.

Printed in Great Britain
by Amazon

47512247R00063